THE BIG ROLES SLAVES PLAYED IN THE ANCIENT AFRICAN SOCIETY

HISTORY BOOKS GRADE 3

CHILDREN'S HISTORY BOOKS

Baby Professor
EDUCATION KIDS

Speedy Publishing LLC
40 E. Main St. #1156
Newark, DE 19711
www.speedypublishing.com
Copyright 2017

All Rights reserved. No part of this book may be reproduced or used in any way or form or by any means whether electronic or mechanical, this means that you cannot record or photocopy any material ideas or tips that are provided in this book.

In this book, we're going to talk about the role of slaves in ancient Africa. So, let's get right to it!

Sometimes when we think of "slavery" the first history that comes to mind is the slavery of African-Americans in the United States before the Civil War. However, that's not the only time that slavery was part of a culture. Slavery was very common throughout the world's history. Surprisingly, this was also the case in ancient Africa.

The African people enslaved their own people. However, the Africans didn't see it that way. When Africans enslaved other Africans they were enslaving people who were not from their specific ethnic or cultural group. Across the African continent, slavery was a way of life in most empires and civilizations during ancient times.

The work that slaves performed and the way they lived their lives was important to the culture and history of the empires of ancient Africa. Over 30% of many different populations throughout Africa consisted of slave labor. Slaves were thought of as the lowest caste or social rank of the population. However, the roles and positions slaves filled, and the rights they had, varied depending on the village and society they lived in.

SLAVES WORKING ON THE COTTON PLANTATION, MISSISSIPPI RIVER

BURNING OF A VILLAGE IN AFRICA,
AND CAPTURE OF ITS INHABITANTS.

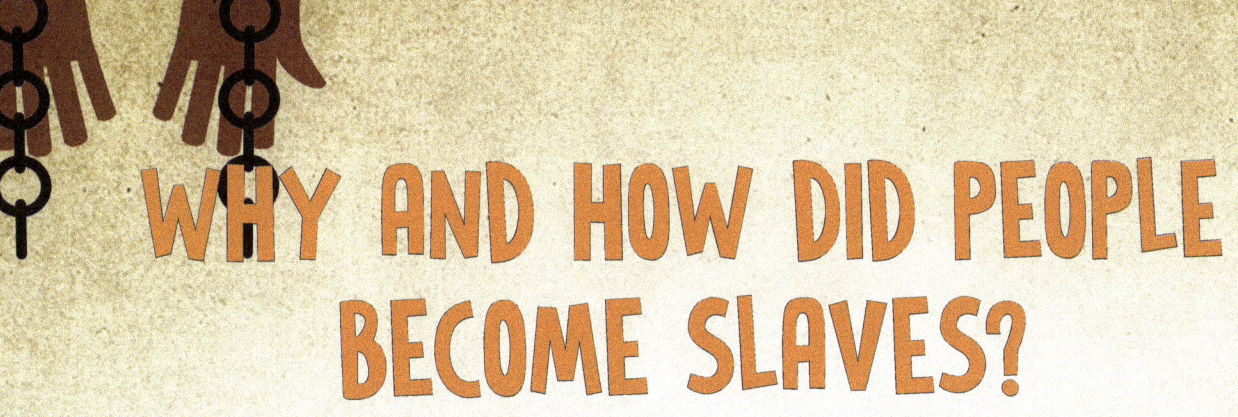

WHY AND HOW DID PEOPLE BECOME SLAVES?

There were many reasons that people became slaves. Sometimes tribes fought and when a particular tribe was victorious, the other tribe that lost would become prisoners or slaves.

These war prisoners were sometimes sold to people in far distant lands so they would not be available to fight again in their homeland. Another reason that people became slaves was to pay off their debts. Sometimes they were criminals and were forced to become slaves to serve time for their crimes. In some societies, children who were born to slaves were also designated as slaves and couldn't become free.

WHAT TYPES OF JOBS DID SLAVES HAVE?

Slaves were often forced to work at the most difficult and physically taxing jobs. They had to do the heavy lifting and carrying on farms as well as the actual planting and reaping.

During this time, there were no machines to help, so it was backbreaking work under the hot, African sun. Some trusted slaves became servants in households where they were tasked with all different types of domestic duties. They carried heavy goods from one location to another.

Plantation slaves

P erhaps the harshest conditions were when they were sent to work in the salt mines of northern Africa. The work was so difficult in these mines that the slaves that were sent there didn't live very long.

Getting sent to work in the mines was essentially the same as being told they were going to be executed. It was just a question of time before their bodies would be too weak to continue to stay alive.

HOW WERE SLAVES TREATED BY THEIR MASTERS?

In some cultures, slaves were treated well, and were almost considered members of the families they lived with. However, in many societies, they were treated as if they were animals or objects.

A PHOTO OF SLAVES THAT WERE TREATED LIKE MEMBERS OF THE FAMILY.

They were considered to be the property of their masters and were severely beaten if they didn't fulfill their master's expectations. They were required to work very hard. Every society was different in their rules regarding the types of rights slaves had. In most cases, they had few if any rights.

THE SLAVE TRADE

The trading of slaves for profit was a main portion of the economy of Africa beginning in 700 AD. The history of the slave trade in Africa is organized into two events.

SLAVE TRADE BY ARABS

SLAVE TRADE BY THE ARABS

Over time, as the Muslims conquered a great portion of northern Africa, they began a very active slave trade around 700 AD. Native Africans, especially from Central Africa, were captured by the Arabs.

They were then transported over the Sahara desert to the Mediterranean where they were bought and sold like property in the slave markets. From there, slaves were often sent to the Middle East and sometimes to Asia. During the time that the Arabs were in power, selling native Africans became a large segment of the continent's economy over hundreds of years.

Slaves transported

SLAVES TRANSPORTED TO A EUROPEAN SHIP

SLAVE TRADE BY THE EUROPEANS

Europeans from different countries arrived in Africa around 1500 AD. The slave trade in Africa had been established for many centuries and was thriving. The Europeans wanted slaves for themselves as well as for the new territories in the Americas. This was a completely new market that required millions of additional slaves.

The European slave trade took place on the western coast of Africa. As the Europeans continued to expand and gain new lands, there was an increasing demand for slaves. Merchants who bought and sold slaves were traveling to the deepest parts of Africa to capture natives to be sold in the markets. It's believed that over 12 million natives were sold as slaves to become the property of masters in Europe and America in the three centuries from 1500 through the late 1800s.

Slave auction

Abolition of Slavery

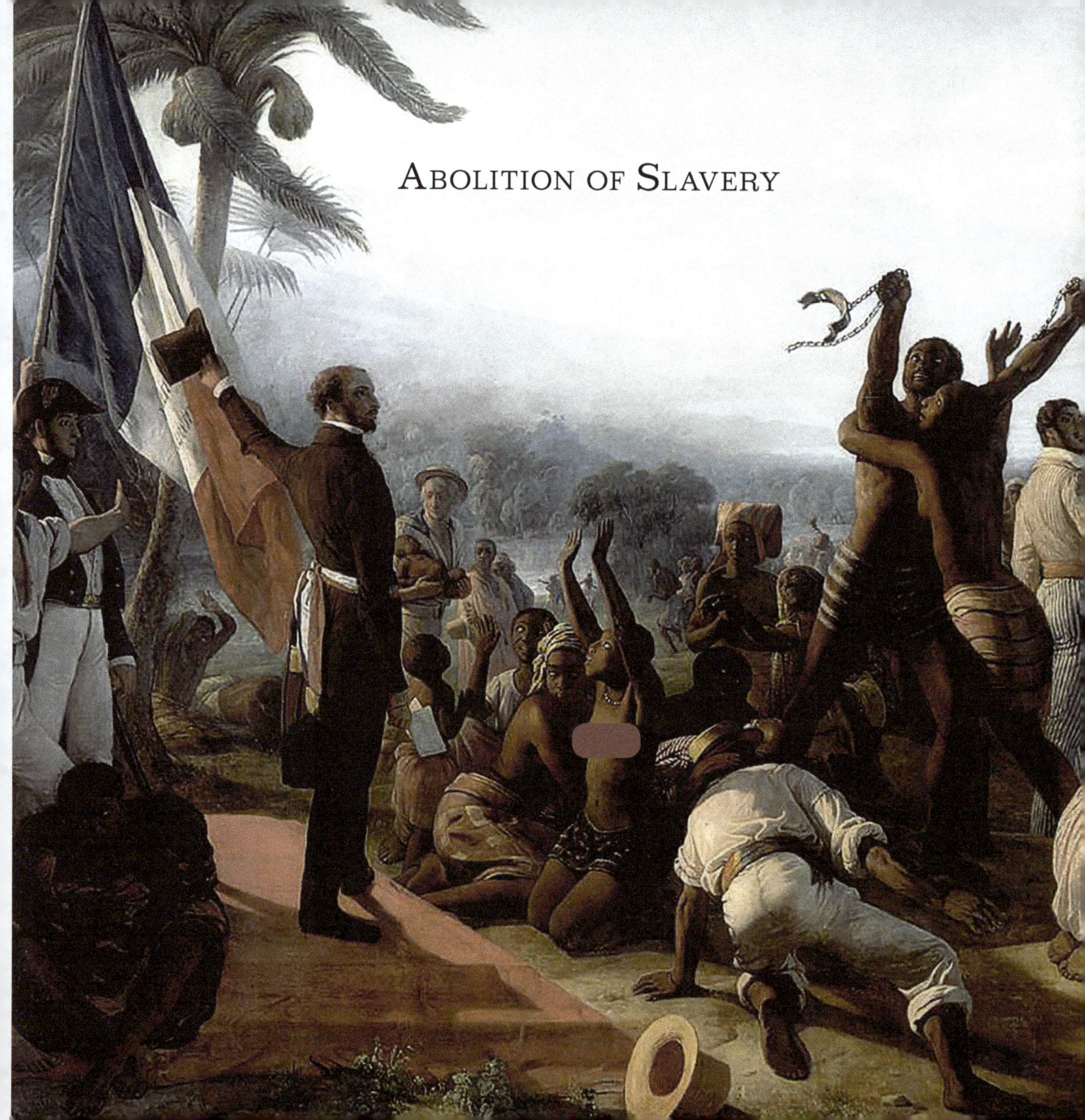

WHEN DID SLAVERY IN AFRICA END?

In the 18th century, Western Europeans began to change their feelings about slavery during the Age of Enlightenment. Slavery was seen as inhumane due to this shift in philosophy and thinking. There was an economic shift during this time as well. Europe was moving from a farming economy to an industrial economy. These changes prompted a movement to ban the practice of slavery throughout the Western world.

Britain began by outlawing the trading of slaves in 1807. The United States followed by prohibiting the trading of slaves in 1808. However, having slaves was still considered legal in the United States. Slaves were smuggled into the US until after the Civil War. Britain further extended their decision to end slavery by prohibiting the practice of slavery in all their territories worldwide by 1833. France followed suit and abolished the slave trade in their colonies by 1848.

After the Civil War, the United States adopted the 13th Constitutional amendment in 1865, which ended the buying, selling, and owning of slaves in the United States. The European, also called the Atlantic, slave trade didn't completely end until the year 1888 when the South American country of Brazil finally prohibited the slave trade. They were the last New World country to end slavery.

Although the European slave trade was beginning to wind down by 1850, other segments of the trade were at their height. The Ottoman Empire, which was ruled by Muslims, tried to outlaw slavery throughout the Islamic world around that same time. However, their rulings had a minor effect.

Hands of a Freed slave

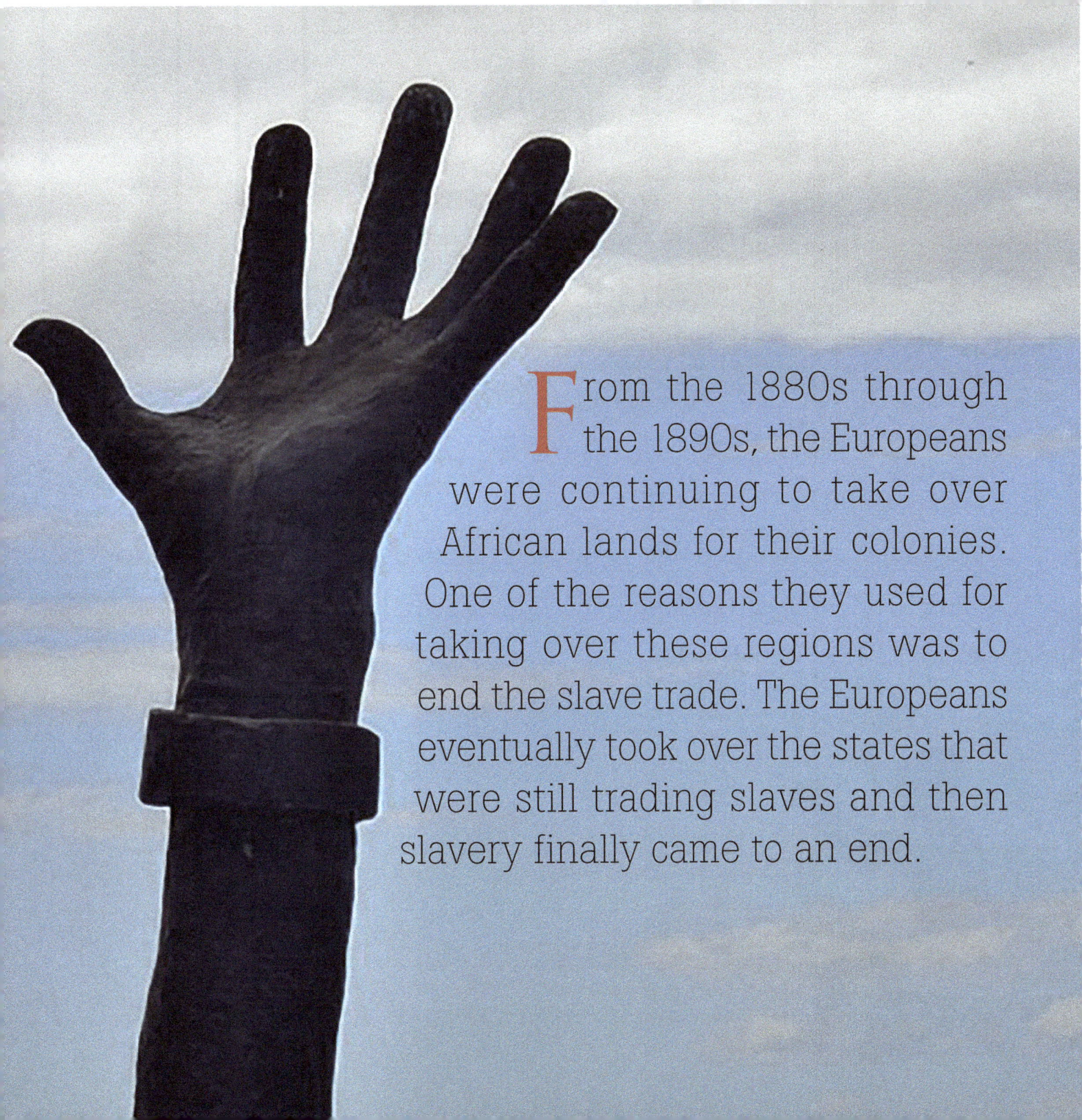

From the 1880s through the 1890s, the Europeans were continuing to take over African lands for their colonies. One of the reasons they used for taking over these regions was to end the slave trade. The Europeans eventually took over the states that were still trading slaves and then slavery finally came to an end.

However, it was not until the 1930s that trading in slaves stopped in Africa. There are many reasons for this, but the major reason is that slavery had been going on for centuries. Trading slaves was a way to get wealthy and when that way was no longer available, the overall economy suffered.

Slaves made it possible for work of all types to be done quickly. Businesses were profitable because the owners didn't have to pay for their workers. The practice of slavery continued illegally and slaves who became free often escaped and went to the colonial authorities. Even though it was no longer legal to keep slaves, many former slaves had difficulty changing their status in society. They were still being looked at as slaves.

The new European colonies in Africa still needed laborers for their farming and industry projects. African leaders, colonial government officials, and former slave masters found ways to get native Africans to work for them for little or no pay.

They said that slavery wasn't legal anymore, but they were still putting native Africans in a position that wasn't much different from slavery. Many descendants of slaves had to live with the pain of slavery for many generations after slavery had been prohibited.

Facts About Slavery in Ancient Africa

When slaves were transported to America on ships they were packed in tight, unsanitary conditions. Over 10% perished on their way to the Americas.

During the 1800s, native Africans feared for their lives on a daily basis. They never knew when they could be captured and forced to become slaves.

Many African leaders as well as warlords and merchants became wealthy by selling other Africans into slavery.

Sometimes slaves escaped to freedom and changed their station in society. Around 1200 AD, Mansa Sakura, who had been a slave, became free and eventually gained the position of emperor of Mali.

Slave escaping

In some societies, certain types of slaves had the right to own property including their own slaves.

House Slaves in Brazil

As the trading of slaves became profitable, and the traders were becoming wealthy, wars were begun with the goal of capturing slaves to bring to market.

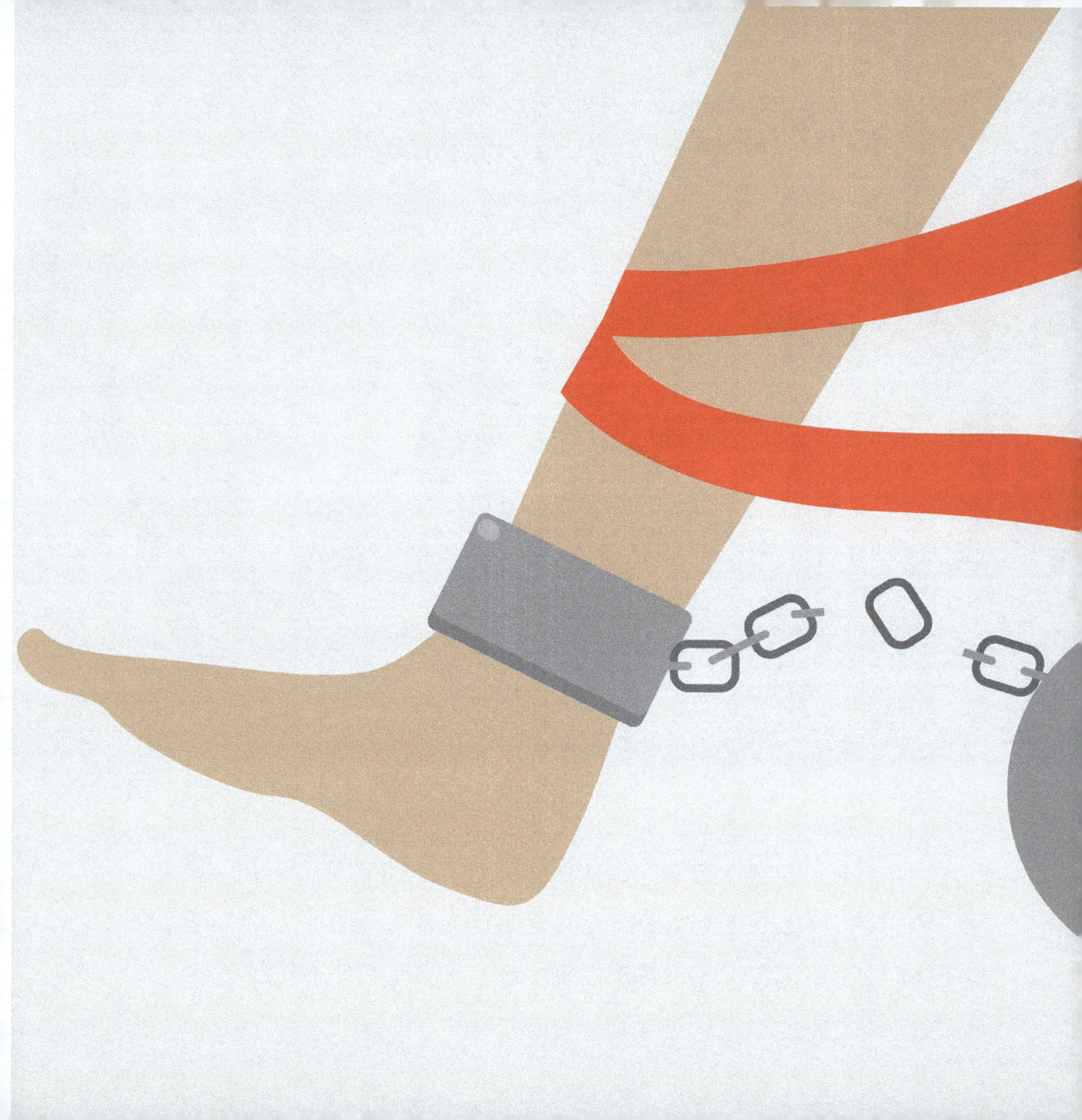

Now you know more the role of slaves and the slave trade in ancient Africa. You can find more History books from Baby Professor by searching the website of your favorite book retailer.

Lightning Source UK Ltd.
Milton Keynes UK
UKHW052158150421
382067UK00005B/44